How To Defend Yourself;
Self-Defense for Men and Women, Real World Self-Defense, Fast, Easy-to-Learn Moves to Save Your Life

By Tony Walker

All Rights Reserved. No part of this publication may be reproduced in any form or by any means, including scanning, photocopying, or otherwise without prior written permission of the copyright holder. Copyright © 2016

Table of Contents

Introduction

Chapter 1: Becoming More Aware

Chapter 2: Managing The Fear Factor

Chapter 3: Controlling Adrenaline and Nerves

Chapter 4: Switching It On

Chapter 5: Your Maximum Impact

Chapter 6: The Various Self Defense Styles

Chapter 7: Your Natural Weapons

Chapter 8: Waking Up for Survival

Chapter 9: Creating Defense

Chapter 10: The One Punch Finish

Chapter 11: Signs Before an Attack

Chapter 12: If it All Goes Wrong

Closing

Introduction

Firstly, I'd like to thank you for purchasing my book *How To Defend Yourself; Self-Defense for Men and Women.*

I'm going to jump straight into the main question here. How would you manage if you were attacked today? Almost certainly when you least expected it? Do you wish you knew about self-defense and how to defend yourself? Would you like to know how to spot a would-be attacker approaching you?

These are the questions I intend to answer in this book. Knowing a few tricks and easy-to-learn moves to get you out of trouble could save your life, and this book has been written to give you an insight into what to do should that need arise.

Violent attacks, muggings, robbery, road rage and rape are on the rise. You only have to look at the newspapers, news channels or more commonly, the newsfeeds on Twitter and Facebook, to see another meaningless assault on some poor victim. Worse still, you may see a video of someone being attacked and passersby refusing to intervene. People prefer to mind their own business than risk getting involved in something unknown.

This puts the average person in no doubt that if something happened, more than likely, you'd be on your own. If we look at the US, there is a 9% spike this year (2016) for violent crime. In the UK for example, 33 of 43 Police Forces have posted a rise in crime. That's a considerable rise throughout the country. How would you manage if you were attacked today walking to work, from work, going to your car? When you least expected it? Not too bad? Okay? Would you freeze? What if you had a loved one with you?

These are very real questions that you should know before anything like that happens. More importantly, could you have seen someone acting in a way that would mean you could have avoided the whole encounter?

It sounds like a would-be attacker has everything in their favor? Well, I'm here to tip the scales back in your favor by showing you what to look for and how to defend yourself. This is for anyone that wants to gain more knowledge on how to defend themselves fast and effectively if a violent attack occurs. These approaches apply to both men and women who want to defend themselves.

I wanted this book to be a quick and easy read in order to give you an easy-to-follow-and-practice strategy that will stay with you forever – which is exactly what you need to survive on the streets.

It would be quite easy to write hundreds of pages noting every type of martial arts move and every type of counter move. This book would be hours long, and by the time I reached the end, you would've forgotten most of what I've said. It is however vitally important to know both effective areas of defense and attack, and I also dispel a lot of myths about the way self-defense is meant to work. I go into the reality of a fight – and into why certain martial arts moves wouldn't work in "real world" scenarios, the specific details on areas of attack, along with information on the inherent risks in attacking such areas.
You are very busy with work and life and the key to self-defense is simplicity.

As I said, I will go into what to look for in suspicious people, and when a person will potentially attack – which is often the best method of self-defense, rather than engaging.

These are techniques that are easy to learn and remember, which can be quickly put into practice should the need arise.

Chapter 1: Becoming More Aware

No one actually wants to fight – well, no normal person does anyway. But sometimes, someone for whatever reason will come at us in our lives, and at that point we need to think fast. Maybe the fight just crept up on you; they provoked you or you provoked them. But knowing how to walk away from a fight can be the most mature and responsible thing you have ever done in your life.

It won't be the easiest thing to do though, and you'll need to stay strong in the aftermath of letting go and not keep bashing yourself for 'not doing something'. Walking away unharmed is a victory in that you are safe.

By becoming more aware of your surroundings, you can learn to avoid getting yourself into situations that could turn nasty. Danger signs include the building up of high tension with someone. Is someone having a rant in a pub about things you care about? Combine that with the presence of alcohol, being overly tired and upset over something else and we have all the ingredients for a likely explosive situation. Some people feel the need to get involved in others' business. Is this you? Sometimes, ignoring or accepting someone else's opinion can give you a calming effect. It's their opinion after all, not yours. What does it truly matter? In two hours you won't even see that person again.
The key is not to get involved in someone else's issues. You don't know what causes them to think the way they do, and by getting involved in a heated debate you become a target for their emotions.

Anger, panic, fear, and frustration are all emotions guaranteed to cause you to fall apart and see red rather than think clearly about what is happening.

If you are caught in the crossfire, attempt to defuse the situation as soon as it arises. The other person is likely as irritated and angry or afraid as you are, and this can make things volatile. Step back or stand away, you make the first call to not engage any further. Keep your distance, and if the other person comes closer, move away again.

Road rage is another flash point. Someone cuts in front of us and we take that as a personal attack on our space. Take a moment to calm yourself. Breathe in and out slowly. The person in front will be out of your life in less than 5 minutes.

It is part of our fight or flight mechanism to escape the situation as quickly as possible if we think we cannot win a fight. However, this is not always possible. There may come a time when you are backed into a corner with no escape possible, and a very angry person waiting to do you harm.

Usually, we assume that this only relates to street fights, and many of us would never find ourselves in an all-out brawl. But in reality, the newest trend is a sneak attack. Youths are running up on people and punching them with so much force they are knocking them out with one punch. It's a scary thought that you could get hit for no reason and be left lying in the street helpless and unprotected.

So what can you do to prevent being attacked, or at least how do you handle it well? The first thing you can do when you feel that you will definitely be attacked is to be in a heightened state of awareness. This is not to say you should walk around paranoid. Instead, pay attention to how the person is standing, or moving towards you. Can you tell which hand they lead with? If you can, then you have a good idea of which hand to move away from when they swing. If you can avoid getting hit entirely then you will inevitably embarrass the person who started the altercation, as well as wear them out. Once they get tired, they may begin saying some nasty things to attempt to get you amped up for retaliation. Do not take the bait. Look for a way to walk away safely and get to a crowed area.

Once you are on high alert for the person trying to attack you, you should take a balanced fighting stance. The key word is *balance*. In order to get the optimal opportunity to dodge any punch thrown at you, you will need to make sure you can stay on your feet. Begin by standing with your feet shoulder-width apart and at an angle. Turn your body sideways so it is less exposed and the attacker has less room to hit any vital areas. You should have your lead foot in front and your back foot straight. Finally, in a relaxed manner, bend your knees.

The idea is that if someone pushes you, you should be limber enough to simply take a step back as opposed to falling over. Also, by shifting your body you minimize the amount of unprotected body area that they have to try to hit. Bending your knees may seem awkward at first, but practice looking like a boxer. You should be able to shift your weight from one foot to the next without feeling unbalanced, and still have the speed to continue moving until you find a way to escape.

Chapter 2: Managing The Fear Factor

Imagine walking down the street in a dangerous area at night, alone, wearing a valuable watch, sneakers, jacket etc. You notice there is an alleyway connected to the sidewalk. Do you cross the street to avoid it? You could walk faster to avoid any interaction with the alleyway and whatever could be around the corner, or you could stop altogether. Clearly, stopping in this situation and hanging around here is not the best idea. However, the thought of freezing could be very appealing if you hear noises? Perhaps drunken yobs coming towards you from the alleyway. Then what? What if they were just some party-goers after a great night?

Fear is something that can creep up on us, and we immediately think the worst of the situation. It's because we have an inherent fear of the unknown. Fear of thinking we can't cope with this. I wasn't trained for this, or shown how to react or behave in this situation. It's the fear of not being in control.

If you have never been in a physical altercation, you are afraid of what could happen and how bad it could be. This jumps straight to the front of our minds. So you stand there transfixed and do nothing – which is exactly what an attacker wants you to do.

For the record, getting hit does hurt. Depending on where you're hit, the pain will be minor or intense. But the simple fact is that it is a painful and unpleasant feeling. If you choose to do nothing, you are putting yourself in more danger than if you fought back. An attacker doesn't want to get hit and will test your fear level.

When you are in these situations, it is imperative to breathe. This sounds simple, but when you are afraid it is one of the hardest things to do. Breathing at a regular pace allows you to focus, not on your fear, but on a solution to getting away from your fear. Being frozen in place by fear should give you a chance to find a way out. Other than finding a way out, you have to snap out of it. You cannot stand paralyzed by the what-ifs that you are facing.

Another key response to fear is to start moving. When you are frozen in fear you are waiting for the negative inevitable. However, if you keep moving, you are helping your body channel your adrenaline from fear to action. You are basically pumping yourself up for whatever comes your way. This is like a fighting work out. Whatever is happening around you, with your heightened sense of your surroundings and your balanced stance, you are ready. This is not to assume that you can beat anyone who attempts to do you harm for any reason. But this process of breathing and moving will help you get over the fear of the possibilities.

Many times we are stressed because we do not have a clue of how things will go. We cannot picture anything positive coming out of being attacked. At times this rationale will help keep us calm and out of harm's way. Once someone has decided that you are their target, you must back up slowly, hands up high, level with your neck, palms open. This is so you can defend yourself, but you're also putting up a barrier in front of you – the first step to regaining your fear. This is controlling fear. Keep breathing. You are taking back control of yourself rather than waiting for what might happen. You are now preparing, your mind on backing up and trying to pacify the situation, but now ready to react.

Chapter 3: Controlling Adrenaline and Nerves

People are emotional beings. When we are not in control we often blame it on our hormones, but what if the statement had more truth to it than we ever thought possible. Controlling your adrenaline is actually controlling your hormones. Adrenaline is a chemical produced by your adrenal glands. When you are placed in dangerous situations, your body pumps adrenaline directly into your bloodstream.

Adrenaline takes a few moments to kick in, but when it does, it can send a mix of emotions and body reactions. Many people feel as though they are moving extremely fast or that everything else has slowed down around them. You can also develop tunnel vision. This is when you are so focused on whatever caused the adrenaline rush that you have a hard time paying attention to anything else happening around you. When the adrenaline is caused by something like stage fright or a fear of heights, you may feel sick to your stomach, weak in the knees, or even freeze in place. Although we already discussed breathing through your fear, it is important to keep in mind that you may still freeze in spite of your pre-planning and technique.

The easiest way to control your adrenaline and nerves is to learn to use them in your favor. If you do not properly understand how adrenaline works when you are fearful, if an emergency happens you will have no way to combat its possible negative effects. In a street fight situation, adrenaline can cause you to panic. This can lead to missed strikes and frantic, unproductive swings. To have a series of unproductive swings is called flailing. This is what many people make fun of when they see fights – two people swinging their arms as if they are swimming.

It is important to accept that freezing is a natural part of having an adrenaline rush. What is more important is what you do with the adrenaline. First you need to make a decision as to what your response will be. Then start moving. When your adrenaline kicks in, it will boost the choice you have already made. An example is if you have decided to swing, you may connect your punch with a little more intensity because of the added strength behind the swing.

Another way to control your nerves is by painting and exploring scenarios. We are not talking about impossible scenarios, but things that could happen at any given time, without warning. Then throw in an event or change that would make your heart race. An example is hypothesizing that while you are jogging, someone runs up behind you and tries to bring you to the ground. You would start paying more attention to your surroundings and be more aware to possibly change your route more often. The idea of controlling your nerves and adrenaline lies in being prepared. If you can conquer your own mind and preparedness, an adrenaline rush will only serve you well when needed.

Chapter 4: Switching It On

Being more switched on is about living in the moment. It is about paying attention to the little things that build a situation. Did you hear the man get frustrated that he dropped his bags of groceries? Did you see the kids laugh at him as they walked by? Did you realize that you kicked his jar of peanut butter by mistake when you walked past? Now, if you had paid more attention you would realize why you are confronted by an angry man. By being more aware of what is going on around you, you could've avoided the whole encounter, and indeed helped the man with his spilled groceries.

Just as we discussed using your adrenaline to work for you, this is the time where an adrenaline surge can really help. By being switched on, when your adrenaline kicks in and everything slows down, you will have a better chance at remembering exactly what was happening around you in that moment. By remembering or even seeing things as they happen, you will have a sense of being more powerful because you are able to react before you know for sure what will happen next. If you are not switched on, you are not paying attention. In a fight this can be the difference between being badly beaten and ending a fight before it even gets started.

Being switched on can also be helpful because even though we are preparing you to be able to physically defend yourself in the event you are attacked, you should keep in mind that not all fights necessarily have to end in violence. If you are switched on you may see through what is right in front of you and be able to be more intuitive with the person who clearly has a problem. Many issues can be solved by communicating properly. This is not always the case, but it is worth the shot, especially if you have never been in a fight and you are not anxious to earn your badge of honor.

When you are switched on, you take time to breathe and allow time between thoughts and actions. You will focus on the present and not concern yourself with the past or future. If you lost a fight last week, that does not mean you will lose one today, and it also does not mean you are doomed to continue getting beaten in the future. Focus your intentions and your energy on the matter at hand and you will be more switched on.

Chapter 5: Your Maximum Impact

Maximum impact when it comes to fighting is all about the follow-through. There are a few points that will help you when it comes to ensuring that each strike that lands is meaningful and felt, and also that each strike that misses its target does not completely throw you off balance. We do not want to see you fighting like the three stooges; this is about protecting yourself, especially when it is needed most.

The first part of creating maximum impact is to actually land your strikes. A major part of this is to not telegraph your punches. This means that the attacker should not have an idea of where you are going to swing before you do it. When we are aiming at something, it is only natural to fix our sights on what area it is that you are going for. If your attacker is paying attention they will notice and will have ample opportunity to change positions or block your advances. The best thing you can do is maintain a loose form of eye contact and keep moving so they are thrown off by your swings.

Another way to have a strong impact is by holding your fist in a way that can cause more damage. My favorite example of how to position your fist is to use the "Frog" punch. When you were a child, if a friend ever punched you in your arm or leg to give you a "frog" or muscle spasm, you know the pain it can bring. In reality, it is using your middle knuckle when making contact with an area. It creates a muscle spasm that only goes away with time but has the same effects as a Charlie horse. Keep in mind that if you are going to use this method, you have to commit to it or you can hurt yourself in the process, and that would be counter-productive.

Finally, to provide yourself with the ultimate level of impact, you need to learn the follow-through. This means that you have to commit to an attack. Regardless of what or how that attack presents itself, you have to give it your all. In Chapter 1 we discussed you having the proper stance in order to keep your balance and continuing to move to find an escape. This can be used with gaining impact as well. When you decide to strike your attacker, you want to use shorter swings and throw your body weight into the punch as well. Using shorter swings gives the opponent less time to react, and you, more time to recover. By throwing your entire body into the punch, you are using your weight and momentum to exert as much energy as you can create. If you swung from further away, the amount of time it takes to connect the punch would make it lose some of its power. Also, by the time you complete a larger swing, your attacker could have already hit you multiple times. This is the one time it is okay to think like a boxer.

Chapter 6: The Various Self-Defense Styles

Most martial arts instructors will tell you that their form of martial arts is the best for protection. The problem is that many of the moves cannot be translated into a street fight. Street fights are unexpected and unscripted. No matter how often you train and practice a particular move, it does not mean that the move will work when someone is trying to punch you in the face, steal your purse, or pickpocket your wallet.

Therefore, the best form of self-defense that we are willing to support is one that emphasizes a strong combative system. This means that it will work on the street, whether you are running away or staying to fight. Combative systems focus on survival, not necessarily winning or losing a fight. That means that it will teach you how to fight dirty. Although, we have been trained to always play nice with the other kids, when someone is threatening your safety, they have given up the possibility of being treated like a rational person.

The strikes associated with this form should be more focused on dual purpose. Meaning, you should be able to use one strike defensively or if you are trying to get the first hit in, in an effort to end the fight immediately. You should be taught the best way to maintain a natural body posture in order to have some form of comfort so you can remain clear headed and calm during a fight.

So, in some cases, the best form of defense is to strike first. But you would only do this when you have tried and failed to cool the situation down; the person can't be reasoned with. So whilst they are mid-sentence coming at you, back up for a brief second and then strike fast and hard for a powerful strike to the nose.

Here is a list of martial arts that have great techniques for a street fight:

Jujutsu
Jujutsu was developed for disarmed samurai. It's an extremely effective martial arts style against both armed and unarmed attackers. The majority of Jujutsu's moves are throws and joint locks (applying breaking pressure to a joint like an elbow or knee)

Taekwondo
Taekwondo is characterized by its emphasis on head-height kicks, jumping and spinning kicks, as well as fast-kicking techniques. The emphasis is placed on speed and agility.

Krav Maga
The main goal of the Krav Maga is simultaneous defense and attack. Unlike many martial arts styles, Krav Maga's attack and defense are intertwined. Instead of blocking until there is an opportunity to attack, you block in a way that opens up the opportunity for a counter attack.

You also attack target the body's vulnerabilities such as the eyes, face, throat, neck, groin and fingers.

Brazilian Jiu Jitsu
BJJ is undoubtedly one of the most effective styles of martial arts in the world. Pretty much all MMA and UFC fighters have trained extensively in BJJ.

BJJ is a mix of takedowns, ground control, passes and submissions, (as well as defenses to each) to leverage and use proper weight distribution to defeat larger and/or stronger opponents.

More important than any of these techniques is the ability to stick it out in order to survive. A good technique for street fighting is knowing that things can get very ugly, very quickly, and being prepared for that. In order to develop the grit it takes to stick something out until you are rescued, you have to practice remaining in a calm mindset regardless of how stressful your environment is. Many people begin practicing yoga or even meditation. This is not a method for everyone, but if you are trying to stay calm and unstressed in an effort to remain prepared for the inevitable, this way could be a positive change for you.

Finally, do not be surprised if you are being taught some brutal tactics – especially in Krav Maga – in order to get free. This is a defense technique, not Martial Arts. We feel the need to point that out. Martial arts is exactly that – martial arts. Some of the moves are so fluid it is as if you are watching them float away. Combative self-defense however is only about ensuring that you survive. By finding someone who teaches Combative Self-Defense, you can be sure that their main focus is to be sure that you have all the tools to defend yourself.

Chapter 7: Your Natural Weapons

Being engaged in a street fight, or protecting yourself from an attack, can happen in an instant, which means you are free to use whatever is the most natural weapon for you at that time. At times it will be an old-school fight where you will only need your two fists and some upper body strength. Other times you may need some fancy foot work or incorporating your head. Still, more violent occasions can lead to the use of weapons. These are all considered natural weapons.

The truth is that anything that can do damage when that is the intended purpose is seen as a weapon. For example, if your intention is to punch someone in the chest, then your fists have just become weapons. When you are trying to get away from a male attacker and you choose to kick them in their groin, you are using your feet as a weapon.

A note to women who are trying to protect themselves against a male aggressor/attacker: The privates should be your first attack goal – go for his balls with as hard a kick as possible. If you're being grappled, either smash a punch there and grab and crush his private parts. I know that sounds pretty brutal, but trust me, you will want to do this for self-preservation. He will let go, halt for an instant, and that's your chance to run to safety.

Usually, people are distracted by stereotypical weapons such as guns, knives, and Tasers. All of these are weapons, but they are not exactly natural. A natural weapon is an extension of you. So the next time you see someone break a glass bottle and point it at someone, just realize that the unsuspecting person being pointed at is actually being threatened with a deadly weapon.

Your natural weapons can be employed in other methods. Should you be a part of a fight that becomes close range combat, you would be wise to learn a few pain compliance holds. A pain compliance hold is when you are able to use your attacker's body and inability to withstand pain against them. There are a number of different methods, but the major components of this technique are moving an appendage in an opposite way than it is intended to go. The object is to do this without actually breaking any joints or bones.

If pain compliance does not work, many street fights become ground fights. Meaning somehow or another, you and your attacker will both end up on the ground dueling it out. In this position, you can use the ground for leverage in order to maintain the upper hand. Also, you can use any holds or restraints to prevent your attacker from moving or to tire them out. This is also a good time to attempt to disarm them if they are carrying some form of external weapon such as a gun or a knife. In a true street fight, size is not supposed to intimidate you. More than what weapons you are using, willpower and mental strength can help you win a fight.

Natural weapons are whatever you are comfortable using in a pinch that will keep you from being harmed. Keeping that in mind can save your life one day.

Chapter 8: Waking Up for Survival

Regardless of what situation you are facing, the number one goal is always survival. We would like to think that we know how to keep ourselves safe, but this is not always the case. There are a few things that you should never do, think, and feel when you are trying to survive any dangerous or violent situation. These are the no no's for survival.

The first rule of thumb is violence can happen to anyone anywhere. So many times we watch the news and think those things could never happen to us. This is a false sense of security. This is almost the same as feeling invincible. These thoughts and emotions can lead to you being unprepared when something does happen. If you are unprepared, you have already lost the fight, because you are most likely to freeze in a time where you need to take action.

Another bad decision when engaged in a street fight is to believe that people will fight fair. Street fights are not fair. Robberies and muggings are not fair. When these things happen, people are out to create the most damage as possible, and many times there is no evident reason why. Street fights in general are about intimidation and ego. If you allow your ego to get the better of you and think the attacker has to shake your hand before he punches you in the face, you are wrong.

Realizing that there will be nothing remotely fair about fighting, you need to keep your distance if you are trying not to get hit. If you allow your attacker to get too close to you, they will have the advantage of using more force in their blows against you. Also, if they are too close to you, the fight can quickly turn to a wrestling match on the ground. Allowing this to happen can be very dangerous because it gives them another advantage of getting you pinned to the ground which can immobilize you. At that point, even the ground can be used as a deadly weapon with enough force.

Finally, if you judge a fight by the size of your opponent, you may be asking to lose a fight. Bruce Lee was not a large man, but he was fast. Each of his strikes held a significant amount of power behind them. If you were to see him walking on the street you would assume from his body stature that he could not fight, and that it may be an easy win for you. Judging a fight based on the size of an opponent can leave you unprepared for the end result or even the first blow.

Key points to also keep in mind are: never let your opponent know where you plan on striking. Also, do not allow them the first strike. If you do, you will have to be faster and smarter to counterattack. Lastly, the easiest fights to win are the ones that are never started. The best way to keep yourself safe is to only engage in violence when there are no other means of protection from an imminent attack.

Chapter 9: Creating Defense

How do you build a wall around yourself when you are fighting? Building a wall is about distance. Your concern is not how close you can get, but rather, how far away you can keep them. You never want to give up ground in a fight unless it is completely necessary. Therefore, when we say build a wall, we mean keep your circle of power.

Your circle of power should be one arm's length away from your chest. If you feel threatened, hold one arm out straight in front of you in order to prevent anyone from moving any closer to you. If a person steps in the range of your arm's distance, they are in a punching or grappling range. This should be taken as an immediate threat. This does not mean that you have to clobber them at that point though.

You can continue to evade danger by taking a step back and to one of your sides. You never want to step straight back because you will leave yourself unbalanced. However, if you step back and they attempt to follow you, the change in direction may actually cause them to stumble. While continuing to step away from the potential attacker, maintain eye contact and continue talking to them. From this point, the fight has not actually begun and you still have time to defuse the situation.

Lastly, part of building a defensive wall is to actually build a layer of defense between you and your would-be attacker. When you realize that there is a problem that could possibly end in violence, you should get to your feet as quickly as possible if you are not already standing. Stand with your feet shoulder-width apart but comfortable. Remember to bend your knees and not be rigid. Bring your hands up to your waist line. Do not place your hands in your pockets. This will leave you defenseless in case the person decides to swing at you with no provocation. You may place your hands in a slight prayer position as you try to defuse the situation, still maintaining the distance between you and them.

Of all the information in this book, this could be the most vital. Protective stances are not natural to us. Again, we do not assume that people will do harm at any given time for no apparent reason. However, if you begin to think of scenarios in which everyone is not a good guy, you will be accustomed to standing at the ready when someone moves close to your personal space. This does not make you paranoid, this keeps you protected and prepared. These are the two main benefits of following the steps that you have been given. Maintaining your secure wall will continue to protect you even when you do not realize it.

Chapter 10: The One Punch Finish

If you have followed all the steps up until this point and you still find yourself in an uncompromising position and you need to defend yourself, do not worry – there are ways to end a fight quickly and with little effort. I will say that it is imperative to practice some of these moves in a mirror and at full speed so that you have a better idea of what your reaction time is or could be once your adrenaline is running its course through your veins.

There are four key areas to punch a person at full force that will incapacitate them and even make them unconscious. The general area of the first three is the head. The head shot is very popular in street fights for many reasons. First, it leaves a lasting impression. If you get punched in the eye, nose, or mouth there is bound to be bruising and a lot of blood. Also, the head is the most susceptible area for mass damage. Getting hit in the head can cause concussions and losing consciousness. You want to avoid any blows to your head.

The least detrimental of all the areas of the head is the nose. Getting punched in the nose is not very likely to make you or your opponent pass out. It will however cause a lot of bleeding and pain. Pain will incapacitate your opponent for enough time for you to walk away from the fight. It will also give the victim temporary impaired vision.

Next in line from least to most detrimental is the uppercut to the jaw. The mechanics of the punch is simple. By quickly striking under the jaw and driving upward, you force the opponent's head to snap back at a rapid pace, causing them to lose consciousness. A straight jab to the jaw line from the side can have the same effect because the head is spinning so rapidly it throws the person off balance and their brain is unable to process what is happening.

The deadliest head shot is to the temple. To make this punch really work, you have to understand what the temple is. This is the area on the side of your skull about 45 degrees from your ears at about an inch in distance. If you press on this area, it seems pliable, like a soft spot on a baby's head. This target area should be used in extreme circumstances only. You will want to use a straight jab to get the most effectiveness, and follow through with your body weight. The reason this punch area is so high-risk is because one blow to the temple can cause internal bleeding, brain trauma, and could easily cause death. The temple punch will most assuredly create an environment where the person will pass out if executed correctly.

If you just want to end the fight and it is not necessary to cause great harm to the person, you could always aim for the diaphragm. The diaphragm is the area just below the lungs in the center of your chest. By hitting someone in this area you will knock the wind out of them. More than likely, your opponent will not pass out, but they will be unable to move. This will give you time to get the distance that you need in order to end the fight.

Chapter 11: Signs Before an Attack

People attack other people for so many reasons. Usually, if you are the person being attacked, the reason truly does not matter. The fact is that if someone wants to fight you, they will. However, you can get out or dodge before they become completely aggressive if you can recognize some of the signs that someone is becoming agitated or angry and inconsolable.

Not all people express their frustration at things by outward signs of aggression. An example of an inward sign of aggression is headaches to the extent of migraines, shaking, sweating, and a rapid heart rate. These are some of the physical things that a person may be going through before they decide to charge after another person and start a fight. Most of these you will have no prior warning about. However, if you are the person having any of these reactions to a situation, it may be time to walk away and get your thoughts collected. This would be a good time to employ deep breathing as we discussed earlier in order to stay focused and be present in the moment for whatever is going on.

Things that people will actually do that can be a warning sign of when to walk away is anything suspicious or out of the norm. For example, if Todd is a relatively soft-spoken person and he starts raising his voice, he may have reached his boiling point and this is the time to defuse the situation or walk away. Other warning signs are pacing, losing one's sense of humor, and aggressive eye contact. If someone is giving you a lot of eye contact in a pub for example, and it feels threatening, then that is probably a good time to leave, but leave with friends or other people. Many times when someone is angry enough to fight, they will attempt to calm themselves down with an external substance such as liquor, cigarettes, or even food. It just depends on what their substance of choice is that relaxes them.

At this point, you should still be able to defuse the situation. If you are able to notice these signs early then you are way ahead of the game. The key is to recognize what is happening around you. If you can calm the situation, then do it. This is made easier by having a rapport with the person who wants to fight. If this is not the case, get out of the way. Move away from the situation; when at all possible, leave. Just remember to do so carefully. It is never advised to turn your back on someone who wants to do you harm.

Chapter 12: If It All Goes Wrong

It is not cowardly to run. There will be plenty of jokes and laughs about chickening out; however, no fight is worth your life. If you are not sure that you can win, or if you are hurt and unable to continue defending yourself, you will need to get away from the attacker as quickly as possible. Just as in every stage of fighting, there is some technique to retreating safely.

Before your own adrenaline surge kicked in, you should have been looking for proper escape routes. If there is a large crowd, make eye contact with people to see if you can get any help in getting away from the situation. Street fights are a spectator sport. This can make it more difficult to walk away from a fight, but when it is your last option, make it work. Once you have found an escape route, you want to do your best to keep that view open while never taking your eyes off your opponent. If they think they have one moment of you not paying attention, they will exploit it.

Catch your opponent off guard. Use misdirection or say whatever it is that they want to hear to distract them. This is also good for muggings, carjacking, or robberies. The key is to distract them enough that they are not completely focused on you. Once they have broken their concentration, it will be significantly easier for you to get away. If the attacker does swing at you as you are trying to escape, remember the vital areas that will end a fight in one punch. Be very careful not to expose those areas such as your diaphragm or temple. These are some of the areas that if hit can and will incapacitate you, which will make escape impossible.

Finally, if none of the evasion techniques work and you are stuck fighting a person who clearly has the upper hand, it may be time to concede. When animals are put in an impossible position, they have the luxury of playing dead. We do not. However, we can surrender. Put both your hands up as if you are blocking a hit and make it known that you are tapping out. You no longer want to continue the fight. If the person is clearly only out for blood, the best suggestion is to place your body in a fetal position, protecting all your vital organs.

Although this may seem like a horrible way to get out of a fight, it is hard to fight someone who is not fighting back. If you have given them what they wanted in the first place and they are still raging on, there is no need to try to escape. It is clear that they have no intentions of allowing you to leave. Therefore, it is more important to protect your vital organs such as your kidney, liver and head, so that you will not be completely incapacitated.

Closing

Thank you again for purchasing this book!

I hope *Self-Defense* was able to help you gain more knowledge in protecting yourself and loved ones. Not only that, but also to make you more aware of suspicious people and when an attack could be imminent.

The next step is to practice these situations once a week, twice a week or when jogging. Think about what you might do if someone attacked you. Just practice mentally how you would react. Practice physically, throwing punch, a kick, moving backwards hands in front – then throwing a punch to the nose. When you're practicing, visualize an attacker attacking you. Don't simply go through the motions. Practice gets you into a comfortable zone where you won't be shocked with overwhelming fear. So if someone came at you, you could do a fast front kick to the groin and escape. Your mind-muscle connection would be fine. You do it instantly. Thinking about how to react could cost you vital seconds.

Remember these quotes:

'To be prepared for war is one of the most effective means of preserving peace.' –George Washington

'Appear weak when you are strong, and strong when you are weak.' – Sun Tzu

'Know yourself and you will win all battles' – Sun Tzu

Be aware of yourself and those around you. I do highly recommend taking up a martial art or kick boxing to gain knowledge and confidence within yourself. Finally, if you enjoyed this book, please take the time to share your thoughts and post a review on Amazon. It would be great to hear from you and whether you found it helpful, and would be greatly appreciated!

Thank you, good luck and be safe friends!

Tony

All Rights Reserved. No part of this publication may be reproduced in any form or by any means, including scanning, photocopying, or otherwise without prior written permission of the copyright holder. Copyright © 2016

Made in the USA
Columbia, SC
03 January 2025